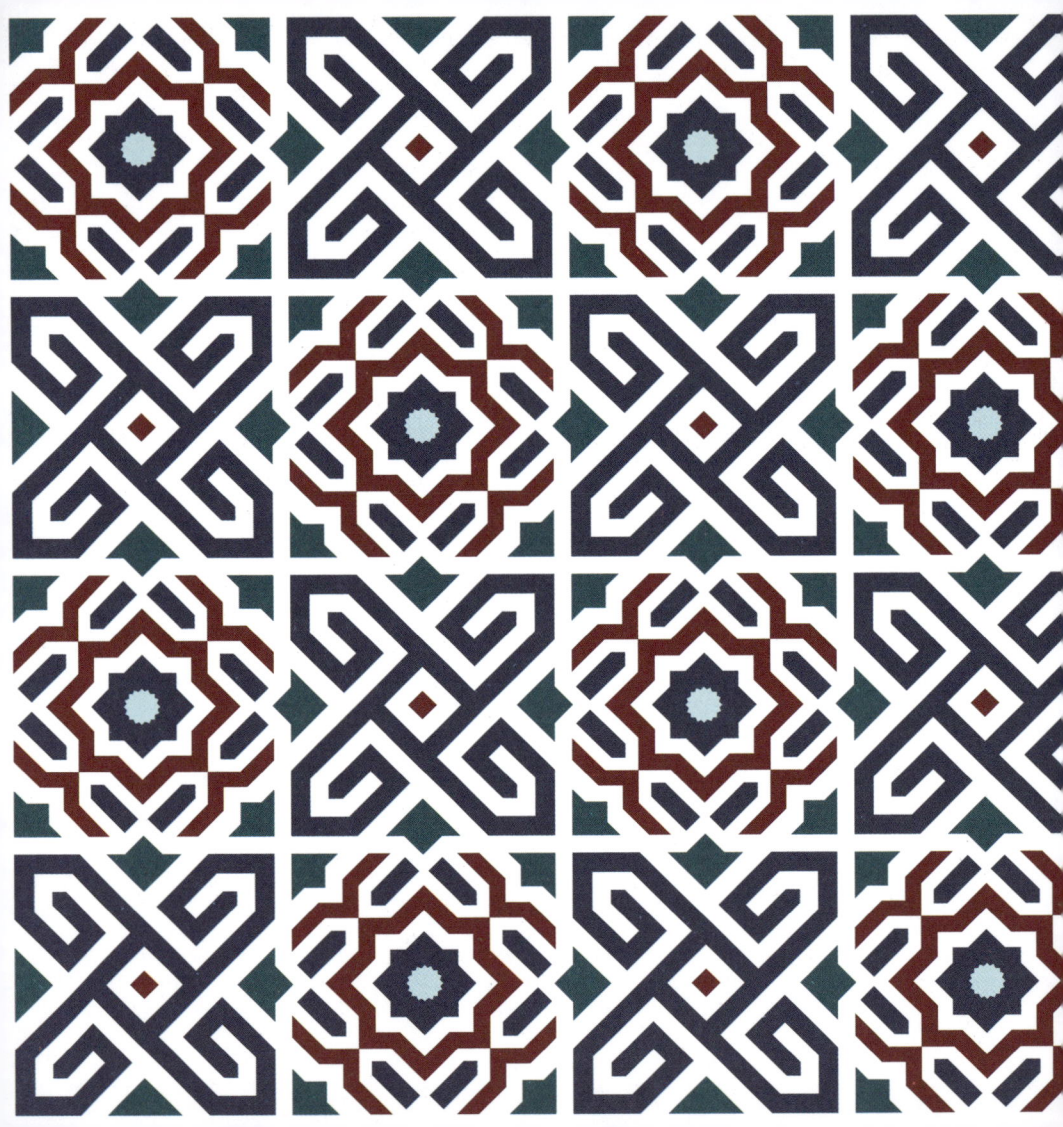

THE BOOK OF UPSIDE DOWN THINKING

BRIAN PATTEN

FOREWORD

I've based many of these rhymes on stories that date back as far as the 11th century and that feature a character little-known in Europe.

In Turkey, he travels under the name of Nasrudin; in Egypt, he's Goha; in Morocco and Tunisia, he's Si' Djeha. Sometimes he's a wise man, sometimes he's portrayed as a fool. Sometimes he can be both at once.

On the simplest level the stories are jokes and anecdotes that help show the world from a different and unexpected perspective. They were often used as teaching stories, containing, if not exactly morals, then certainly wisdom.

While in Morocco last winter I turned some of the stories into verse, adapting some quite substantially. Others are my own invention, inspired by and written in the spirit of Nasrudin. The aim of them all is to rattle the cage of conventional thinking. I hope you enjoy reading them as much as I did writing them.

Brian Patten

ARE YOU ACROSS THE RIVER OR AM I?

I was walking along a river bank.
A man on the other side
Shouted, "How do I get across?"
"You are across," I replied.

VANITY

When I broke the mirror I bought a new one.
I didn't like what I saw,
So I took it back to the shop and asked for one
Like the one I'd bought some years before.

THE DITCH

Every time you see me now
You look at me and say,
"Remember when I dragged you out
That ditch one rainy day?"
You stop everyone who passes by
You point at me and say,
"When he was drunk I dragged him out
A ditch one rainy day."
You tell the tale repeatedly
But sadly there's a hitch-
Life goes on and I've gone on,
But you're still in the ditch.

AT THE BORDER

"You must have some means to identify yourself,"
The officious official said.
I held a mirror to my face.
"Yes, that's me," I said.

SOUND SENSE

I stood outside the baker's shop
And sniffed the scent of baking bread.
"You'll have to pay to smell it,"
The miserly baker said.
I said that was not possible,
I'd given up bread for Lent.
Instead I jingled the coins in my pocket
And paid with sound for scent.

THE PLACE AHEAD

I was standing at a crossroads
When a man came up to me and said,
"Can you tell me what it's like
In the town up ahead?"
I asked him what it had been like
In the town through which he'd passed.
He said it had been a dreadful place.
I said, "You'll find the next place like the last."
Soon after he was gone from me
Another man came by,
He too asked if the place ahead
Was a good place in which to stay.
I asked him what it had been like
In the town through which he'd passed.
He said it had been quite wonderful.
I said, "You'll find the next place like the last."

WHAT THE SHADOW SAID

I went to your house the other day.
Your son came to the door.
I said I'd come to collect a debt
From several months before.
He said you'd left on business,
He said it was a bore,
But if I came back in a week or two
You'd pay me then for sure.
I said you'd be back sooner,
Of that I too was sure,
For you'd forgotten to take your shadow
From behind the kitchen door.

A TEST OF FAITH

A priest stumbled over the edge of a cliff.
He clutched at a vine as he fell,
And there he swung in a terrible limbo
Halfway between Heaven and Hell.
"Dear God," he called, "please help me.
Please rescue me from this!"
He prayed to his God as never before
As he dangled above the abyss.
A voice out of nowhere answered,
"I can see you're a disciple of mine.
My son, of course I'll help you-
But first ... let go the vine."

REVELATION

God giveth and He takes away-
He must have been in church today.
Celestial light upon the alter shone,
But the silver candlesticks were gone.

A HELPING HAND

I saw a tax collector drowning,
I wondered what to do.
I could have looked away
And admired a different view,
But kindness got the better of me:
"Give me your hand," I said.
He found this task impossible,
So I gave him mine instead.

UNWARRANTED CONCLUSIONS

I stood in a bleak cemetery and many a passer-by
Offered up well-meant platitudes
When they saw me stare at the grave and sigh,
"Why did you have to depart this world?
Oh, why did you have to die?"
They explained to me how grief would pass,
They told me to be brave,
And I was too embarrassed to tell them
It was my wife's first husband's grave.

CREATURE COMFORTS

My creature comforts no longer comfort me.
The truth is, they never did.
It was always the thought of leaving them behind
That was the luxury.

A GOOD PLACE FOR SECRETS

A friend wanted me to keep a secret.
I didn't want it festering in my head,
So I took it to a café in the marketplace,
And I left it there instead.

SEEING THE LIGHT

He lost a ring down an alleyway.
He saw no point looking for it there.
The night was black, the alley dark,
He wandered off to look elsewhere.
I saw him under a street lamp
Later on that night.
"Why are you looking here?" I asked.
He said, "Because there is more light."

A PERSON'S VALUE

"How much do you think I'm worth?"
Brayed a dinner guest.
He egged me on to name a price.
He thought I'd be impressed.
His house was worth three million,
His suit was expensive too.
His car was a Lamborghini,
His Rolex looked brand new.
The blonde nailed to his side
Was as classy as they come,
So I studied him and thought a while
And came up with a sum.
I said, "Take away the trappings
And the sum that makes most sense
Is not a million or a billion,
But probably two pence."

SPIDER LAW

"Spider, spider, why is the law
So like a spider's web?"
"It catches flies, but lets the hawks go free,"
Is what the spider said.

A TIP

I went into a restaurant.
They stuck me by the kitchen door.
The soup was cold, the fish was off,
The service was quite poor.
The wine was warm, the waiters rude,
The bread baked the day before.
When I left I tipped them generously,
Far more than they'd expect,
They looked at me with different eyes
And almost showed respect.
I went again the following week.
I was treated like a king.
Everything was perfect.
I couldn't fault a thing.
The soup was hot, the fish was fresh,
The wine the very best.
The waiters were subservient
I really was impressed.
I left a penny tip behind,
They had expected more,
But I said the tip I'd given them
Was for the week before.

IN PLAIN SIGHT

I rode up to the border on my donkey.
The guard pulled me aside.
"What's in those sacks the donkey's carrying?
What have you got to hide?"
I didn't like his tone of voice
Or what his questioning implied.
I said there was absolutely nothing
That I wished to hide.
Still, he searched the creature's panniers,
And it really was a farce
When he snapped on a pair of surgical gloves
And looked up the donkey's arse.
Finally he gave up searching.
He decided what I'd said was true.
He waved me on my way. I smiled,
And smuggled the donkey through.

THE UNTRICKABLE STUDENT

"No one can trick me," said my student.
I said, "Are you sure that's really true?
If you wait here a moment
I'll find a way of tricking you."
So my student said he'd wait,
And for all I know
He might still be waiting for me to trick him,
Though I hope that is not so,
For I left him standing in the rain
Fifteen years ago.

THE CONUNDRUM

I met a magician in the market-place.
"I can teach you to read," he said,
"By simply lifting up my finger
And tapping on your head."
I was in awe of magicians
I paid him a small fee,
Then I bowed down before him
And he worked his magic on me.
Later on I bought a book
And that night in bed
Opening it with trembling hands
I read, and read, and read.
Later still I tossed and turned,
Distraught, I could not sleep.
I flung that book across the room,
All I could do was weep.
How could I have been so gullible?
How could I have been so thick?
The book had clearly stated:
'All magic is a trick.'

WHERE DOES THE MEANING RESIDE?

"They say your jokes are full of hidden meanings."
"That's not exactly true.
Any meanings they might have
Are hidden inside you."

PRIORITIES

Ah the futility of it!
Spending so much time in front of mirrors
When the soul itself is threadbare.

THE EFFICIENT WIFE

My husband was always complaining
That I never thought things through.
He said I was always ill-prepared
No matter what I set out to do.
I did my best to rectify this
The day he came down with the flu.
He sent me to find a doctor,
I decided to come back with two-
One to make the diagnosis
Another to confirm it was true.
I brought an undertaker,
A cleric from the mosque,
A carpenter to make the coffin,
A professional mourner to weep pious sighs,
A couple of gravediggers with their spades-
And two coins for my husband's eyes.

THIS TOO

"Make me a ring that when I'm unhappy
Will also make me glad,
And that in times of joy will remind me
Life can also be sad."
I made her a ring with an inscription
That was as clear as glass.
On its inner rim I had inscribed,
"This too, my love, will pass."

BRICK

He set off on a long journey,
Longer than any he'd made before.
He took with him a few belongings
And a brick from beside the front door.
I asked him why he was taking the brick.
He said if the journey was ever a chore
He'd feel the weight of that brick and remember
The house weighed a thousand times more.

TAKING THE DONKEY'S WORD

A neighbour asked if he could borrow
My donkey for the day.
I didn't like my neighbour,
I said I'd given it away.
"You're a liar," said my neighbour,
"I've just heard the creature bray."
"You mean you understood its braying?
You heard the donkey say it's here?"
"Of course," said my neighbour
"Its braying made that clear."
I said if he believed the donkey's word
Rather than my own
Then he could go and find
A donkey of his own.

PHEASANT

A man was hunting a pheasant,
It scuttered out the way.
"Bravo! That's brilliant," I shouted.
"That's the best thing I've seen today."
"Are you mocking me?" asked the hunter.
I said, "No. I was being pleasant.
Please do not take offence.
I was speaking to the pheasant."

A PRESUMPTUOUS ASSUMPTION

I checked into a fantastic beach hotel.
"We'll make you feel at home," the manager said.
I protested at his assumptions,
Cancelled the booking and fled.
I lived at the back of a car-park
And wanted some glamour instead.

HELL'S COLD TRUTH

A man who lived in a freezing house
Made a brief visit to Hell.
He guessed with so much fire down there
They'd have plenty left over to sell.
The Devil laughed at his request.
He said, "The truth to tell,
All the souls condemned to this place
Bring their own flames to Hell."

THE SCRUFFY TRUTH

I was invited to a posh dinner
But when I turned up at eight
My host said, "You're far too scruffy-
You're not dressed appropriate."
So I went back home. I got tarted up.
I wore a suit fit for a king.
When I returned my host, impressed,
Couldn't have been more welcoming.
So I dipped my tie in the soup,
And my elbows in the fish.
I carefully stuffed my pockets
With bits from every dish.
I buttered both my lapels.
With my cuffs I wiped my plate.
My host looked on in horror,
I thought he'd asphyxiate.
He said, "What are you up to?"
I said, "You made that clear.
It was not me, it was the suit
You invited to dine here."

WHAT THE POOR MAN HAS

I have what men love more than life,
And fear more than death.
I have what the miser spends and the spendthrift saves,
And all men carry to their graves.

INAPPLICABLE GOOD ADVICE

He asked me to look after his donkey,
His ageing mother as well,
He fretted over both of them
And he was going away for a spell.
He was hardly gone before the donkey died.
I sent a note saying, "Donkey's dead."
He berated me for being curt.
"You could have broken the news gently," he said.
His mother died soon after the donkey
And remembering what he had said,
I wrote to him saying she was poorly,
And had a bit of a cold in the head.

DEATH AND SILAS BROWN

Mr Brown heard that Death was coming to his town,
To look for the one man living there
Whose name was Silas Brown.
He sailed to a far-off city
And changed his name to Mr Wright,
Still, Death found him in a dockside café,
Half-drunk in the candlelight.
"Aren't you looking for a man called Brown
In a different town tonight?"
"I am," said Death, "but first of all
I've got to pick up a man called Wright."

WAVES

Even the one throwing the lifebelt
Needs help at times,
Stranded on the beach,
Terrified of the waves.

TOUCHÉ

I saw a child carrying a candle,
I asked him where its light came from.
He blew the candle out and asked
Where the light had gone.

AMOUR

She said I was a wolf in sheep's clothing.
Not true.
I was a lamb in armour.

OWNERSHIP

I saw a thief steal my TV
And take it to his flat.
He stole the cups,
He stole the plates,
He stole the welcome mat.
He stole the bed,
He stole the chair,
And when he came back later,
He stole the mirror and the desk
And the refrigerator.
He went out to a café
And while he fed his face
I used a bunch of skeleton keys
And stole into his place.
When the thief got back home
And found me in the bed
He was annoyed with me
And turned a criminal shade of red.
I said do not worry.
I sleep quiet as a mouse,
And anyway hadn't he
Just moved me to this house?

USELESS THINGS

"People are interested in useless things
Rather than in what's useful and good!"
"Prove it, Nazrudin," said his friend.
Nazrudin decided he would.
He held up a jar in the marketplace.
People ignored it and walked on ahead.
When he smashed it they gathered around to stare.
"There's your proof," Nazrudin said.

WEALTH

"How much money did he leave behind?
He had so much of it!"
"I thought that would be obvious.
He left every single bit."

EXTRA SWEET

I went into a café with a friend
Who was just as poor as me,
Between us all we could afford
Was a single cup of tea.
"Have your half first," he said,
"Then leave the rest for me,
For there's only enough sugar
To sweeten half the tea."
I said I wasn't bothered.
I said it would be fine
For I often liked
A pinch of salt in mine.
He changed his mind immediately.
He dropped the sugar in the tea.
It might not have been sweet enough for him,
But it tasted extra sweet to me.

STITCHING UP THE PHILOSOPHER

"Where are we going?"
The philosopher asked.
I said, "No mortal ever knows.
It might be as far as John O'Groats
Or to Land's End, I suppose…"

SEEING AND NOT SEEING

I saw a blind man on a path
When I walked out one night.
He came towards me silently,
In his hand he held a light.
I asked him what use he had for it
When he had lost his sight.
He said that if I thought a while
The reason would be plain to see.
"It's not to help me on my way," he said.
"It's to stop you bumping into me."

COLLUSION

The dictator is cruel and vain.
He thinks he is still young.
His beard is grey.
His ministers are colour-blind.

SEEKING ANSWERS FROM A BEARD

Seeking answers to life's riddles
A friend took me to see,
A guru with a long white beard
Sitting under a banyan tree.
I was underwhelmed
And did not want to gloat,
But last time I'd seen such a beard
Was on a billy-goat.

NURI BEY

He had been away a year and a day.
When he returned home a servant said,
"There's a trunk large enough to hide a man in
At the foot of your young wife's bed."
It might have been empty, it might have been full,
It might have contained only trinkets and dust,
It might have contained a lover,
Or a whisper of mistrust.
Nuri Bey could have opened the trunk
But, haunted by what the servant said,
He pondered over the problem and then
Had a far better idea instead.
He had the trunk loaded onto a cart.
It trundled off through the pouring rain.
The trunk was buried deep in a wood,
And it was never mentioned again.

HE WENT TO THE FORTUNE TELLER

"You'll be unhappy until you are sixty.
You'll be miserable and unfit."
"Then what will happen after that?"
"Then you'll get used to it."

THE HAMMER'S REVELATION

In the monastery the monk was banging away
Hanging an icon up on the wall.
The place was old, the monk half-blind
And the wall was itching to fall.
He hadn't been out into the sunlight
For sixty years or more
So when a hole appeared in the masonry
He was amazed by what he saw.
There was a garden full of blossoms
Where in his youth a wasteland had stood.
The bees were drunk on pollen
And the world tasted good.
His soul had ached for paradise
For sixty years and a day
And now he'd suddenly discovered
It was the thickness of a brick away.
He praises God for the revelation
And ignoring the work the hammer had done
Singing hallelujahs
He stepped out into the sun.

HEDGING HIS BETS

"You'll pass half your exams with this book.
It'll be pretty useful to you."
"Fantastic," I said, "I'm delighted.
You might as well sell me two."

FISHING FOR FISH

I was fishing on the river bank
When a man came up to me and said
I should be earning a living,
I should be working hard instead,
Then when I'm old, if I'm rich and I wish,
I could be sitting on a river bank
Fishing for fish.

SWEET ADVICE

The angry wasp is in the honey.
Don't fiddle with it.
Let the honey sort it out.

A SELF, SATISFIED

He dreamt he'd won the lottery
And sponsored many a good cause.
He woke up the next morning
Expecting loud applause.

KNOW THE PATIENT

A beggar collapsed in the marketplace.
We thought he might be dead.
One doctor held salts under his nose
Another pressed ice to his head,
But he only revived when under his nose
Someone held a lump of bread.

TWO LEGS OF EQUAL AGE

"The pain in my leg's due to old age?
Doctor, you're a twit!
My other leg is just as old
And it doesn't hurt a bit."

PLANTING SEEDS

Two men saw me kneeling in the garden
When they passed my house the other day.
One said I looked a kindly man,
He'd seen me kneeling down to pray.
The other spread the word I was someone to ignore.
He'd seen me crawling on my hands and knees-
A drunk and local bore.
There was no correcting either man
For both of them had been
Describing something about themselves
Rather than what they'd seen.

AN OPTIMIST IN LOVE

I dreamed you were in love with me,
And desired me as I desired you.
All was not lost when I told you this,
For you said half my dream was true.

A DISADVANTAGE OF OBEDIENCE

He knocked the lid off the coffin.
He sat up and looked around.
There was a funeral taking place
And a deep hole in the ground.
"I'm alive. Alive!" he shouted.
"No, you're not," the mourners said.
"We've a certificate to prove it.
The doctor's confirmed that you're dead.
Stop spoiling the funeral.
Your will's already been read."
He'd always been an obedient man,
Always believed what the experts said,
So he lay back down in the coffin,
And he stayed there until he was dead.

DONE AND DUSTED

The Devil was sitting alone in a café
Idly passing the time of day.
He was sipping a weak Bloody Mary
When a stranger came his way.
"Shouldn't you be out working,
Causing havoc and fuelling sin?"
The Devil turned towards him
And said, with a world-weary grin,
"Souls are mortgaged daily,
On the markets sins accrue,
Malice breeds like blowflies.
I've nothing left to do."

THE WORD SPOKEN IN HASTE

You can catch the word ball
You can dry the word wet
You can thaw the word frost
You can find the word lost
You can calm the word fright
You can light the word night
You can hush the word loud
You can plant the word seed
You can staunch the word bleed
Yet no matter what energy you waste
You can't overtake a word spoken in haste

COUNTING THE STARS

"How many stars are there in the sky?"
The wise man asked the fool.
The fool looked up, he thought a while,
He smiled and then replied:
"There are as many stars in the sky
As there are hairs on my mule's backside."
"That's absurd," the wise man said.
"Prove me wrong," the fool replied.
"First, count the stars in the sky,
Then count the hairs on my mule's backside."

A CLUE

They'd been asking him the name of his donkey for years,
The entire village wanted to know,
But the donkey's name was a secret that he
Was reluctant to let go.
When the donkey died and he buried it
They remained baffled even though
On a slab of stone he had inscribed,
"Here rests my poor Ego."

IT DOESN'T RUB OFF ON YOU

When the great philosopher called on me
Word spread around
That contrary to popular belief
I, too, was profound.
We'd held no deep conversations,
We'd shared no particular views,
He simply lived the right distance from me
To walk over and break in his shoes.

SAVING FACE

I put my right foot in the stirrup on the left side of the horse.
I heaved myself up and had to swallow my pride
When I found myself facing the horse's backside.
Pretending it was normal and not at all perverse
I tried my best to look nonchalant as I shuffled home in reverse.
My neighbours thought me stupid so I said I was intent
On looking back to where I'd come from
Rather than to where I went.

MISUNDERSTANDING THE MOURNERS' INTENTIONS

As the funeral procession passed
One sad and sombre day,
I heard the weeping mourners
Bow their heads and say,
"He's going to a place of darkness
Where there is no food or warmth or light."
And I thought, "Oh, my God!
They're taking the corpse to my house tonight!"

SCUTTERED

The teacher said, "There's no such word as scuttered.
You can't spell things any-old-how."
The student looked at her and said,
"There's a word such as scuttered now."

THE ODDS

I bet the king I could teach the cat to read.
It would take ten years, I said.
"A hundred gold coins if it's possible.
If not, it's off with your head."
When I took an advance on the bet
My wife berated me.
I explained no man could read the stars
Or know his destiny.
The days are brief as grass, my love,
Life hangs by a thread.
In ten years time the king or I,
Or the cat will be dead.

DEGREES OF NOTHING

A rich man prostrated himself on the floor of a mosque.
"I'm nothing, I'm nothing!" he cried.
The mosque was open to the marketplace,
An old beggar limped inside.
He looked for a space between the worshippers,
And propping his crutch against the wall,
Prostrated himself beside the wealthy man
And took up the self-same call.
The rich man turned and stiffened.
His disdain was plain to see.
He smirked and said to his neighbour,
"Look who thinks he's as nothing as me!"

THE REPLY

It's not true to say I did not reply.
I sent no letters back, that's for sure,
But I felt my silence said much more.

THE DONKEY'S HORSE

He had a horse and I had a donkey.
He was haughty and he looked down on me.
One morning when I was sitting beside the village watercourse
He rode past and asked where the donkey was.
I said it was out riding a horse.

ANSWERING A METAPHYSICAL QUESTION

"If donkeys had souls where would they go
When their time came to say farewell?"
"To the place that has the most carrots," I said,
"Whether it's Heaven or Hell."

THE PLACE THE LIGHT ONCE CAME FROM

"Is this what they call a lamp shop?" I asked.
"There are no signs, and the window is bare."
"That what it's still called," said the owner,
"But the light has been moved elsewhere."

IN A BLINK

He arrived outside Paradise on his donkey.
He was surprised he had come so far.
He'd got up that morning expecting
To go to the local bazaar.

RIPPLES

People are writing up their diaries at the day's end.
How can they know so soon what's happened?

First published by Forget Me Not Books, an imprint of from you to me Ltd, May 2018.
from you to me, The Old Brewery, Newtown, Bradford on Avon, BA15 1NF, UK

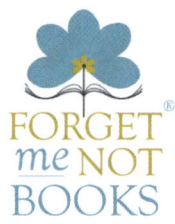

www.ForgetMeNotBooks.com

Published, printed and bound in Spain. This paper is manufactured from
pulp sourced from forests that are legally and sustainably managed.

1 3 5 7 9 11 13 15 14 12 10 8 6 4 2

All rights reserved. No part of this publication may be reproduced, stored in a retrieval
system, or transmitted in any form or by any means electronic, mechanical,
photocopying, recording, or otherwise, without the prior written permission of the
copyright owner who can be contacted at info@rcwlitagency.com.

Illustrations © from you to me ltd
Text © Brian Patten
Brian is available for readings and can be
contacted via his website www.brianpatten.co.uk

ISBN 978-1-907860-10-2

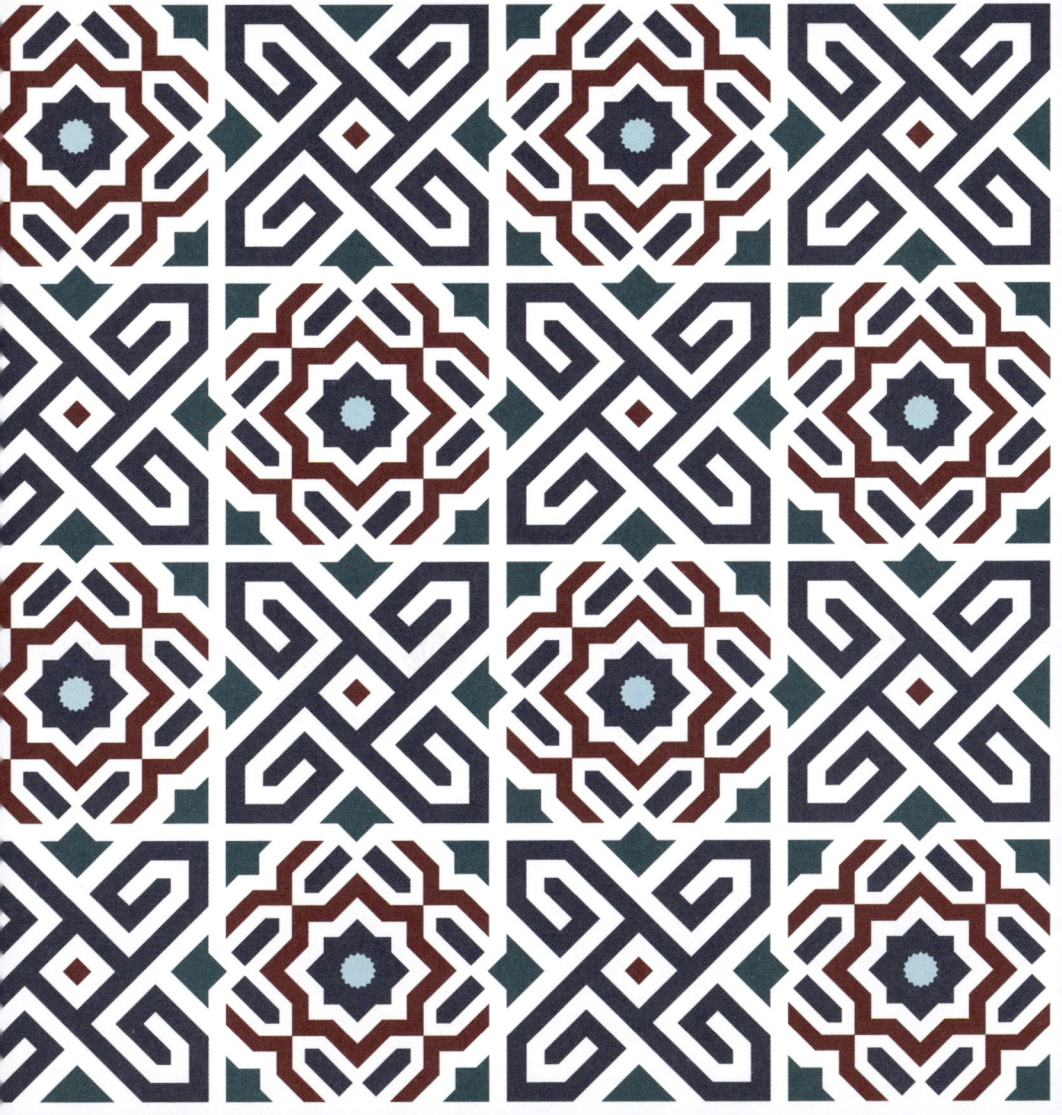

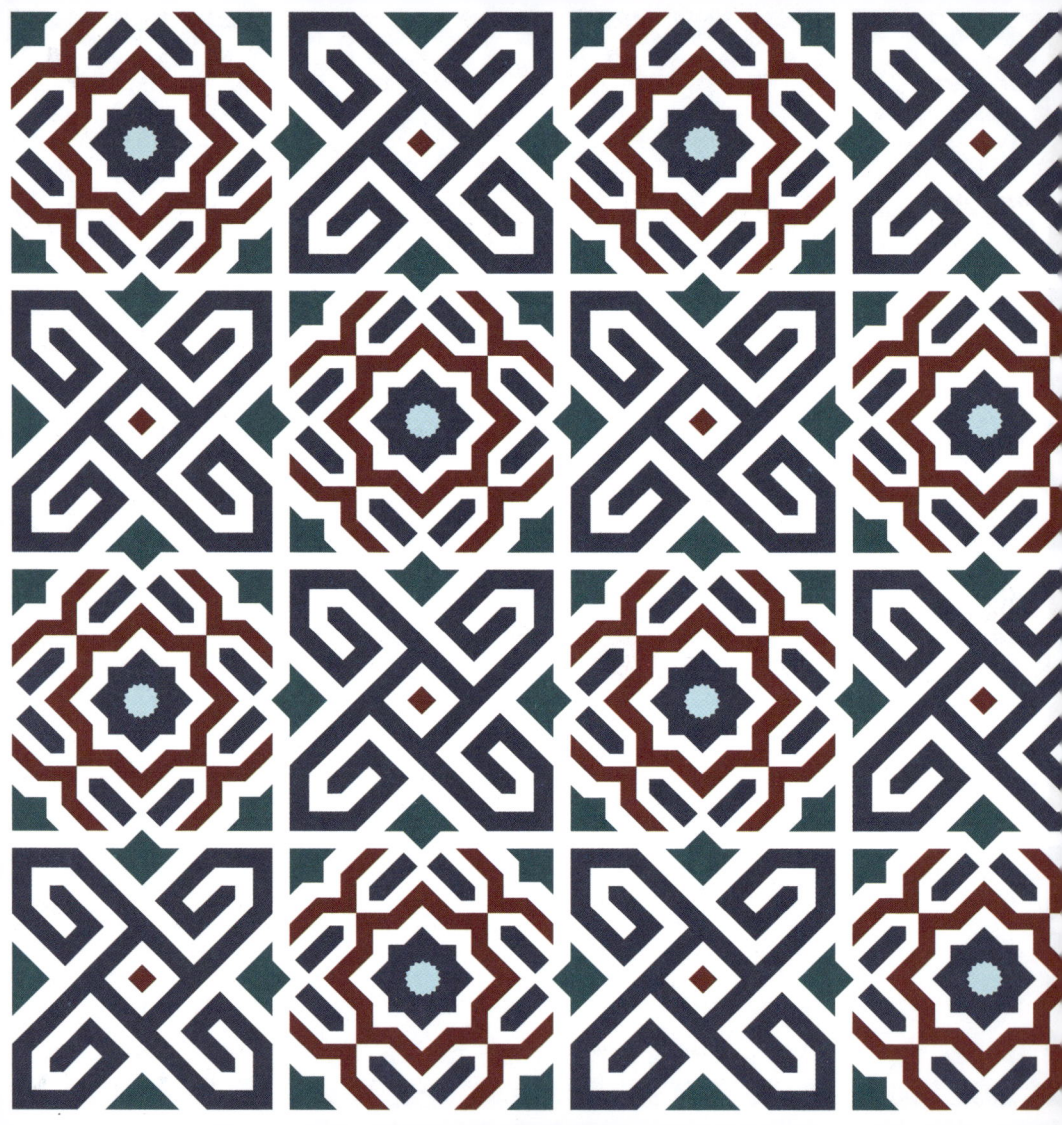